The United Nations
Come along with me!

The United Nations
Come along with me!

by Nane Annan

The American Forum for Global Education

The United Nations is like a club of countries from all over the world.

They have joined together to do many things to help the people of the world.

They call themselves the United Nations.

This building in New York City
is the home of the United Nations

The United Nations tries to prevent wars.

It helps the poorest of the poor.

It watches out for the children of the world.

It wants to make sure that everyone will have clean air to breathe and clean water to drink.

My husband is the Secretary-General of the United Nations.

His name is Kofi Annan.

My husband Kofi Annan

My husband is from Ghana in West Africa.

Ghana was the first country in Africa to become independent from colonial rule.

My husband says it gave him a wonderful sense that everything is possible.

I am from Sweden in the north of Europe.

Together we live in New York, the home of the United Nations.

We feel like a mini-United Nations ourselves.

My journey with my husband started here in New York on our way to be married, a long time ago.

You can see that his hair was still dark then!

Here we are on our way to be married in New York

Since my husband became Secretary-General,
we have gone all over the world.

We wanted to see how the United Nations
is helping people.

We have met the leaders of many countries.

We have met the people living in these countries.

I want to tell you about some of these trips.

You can follow our journey by using the map.

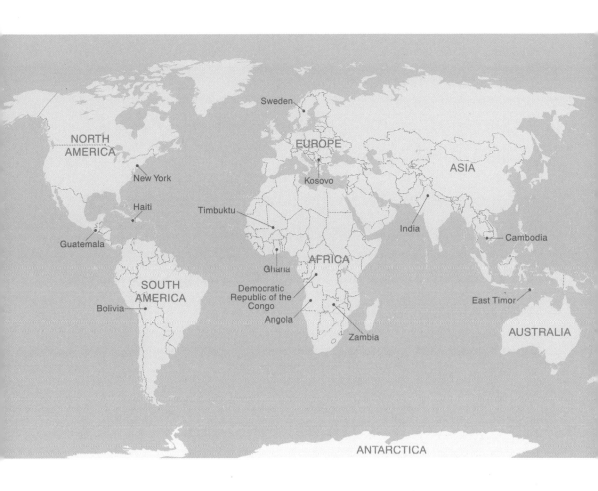

Here are all the places I talk about in the book

We have met so many refugees who are helped
by the United Nations.

Refugees are people who have fled their country
because they fear for their lives.

In Timbuktu in Africa we visited refugees who had
returned to their homes.

They gave my husband a high turban to show how
many problems he has.

They gave me a brown and white cloth to show that
people of all colors have to live together in peace.

We visit Timbuktu

In Europe we met more refugees.

At the border of Kosovo we met this woman.

She was a hundred years old.

She could not understand what had happened.

Why was she so far away from home?

Talking with a 100-year old refugee woman from Kosovo

Wherever we go we meet people working for the United Nations.

Many have given up comfortable lives to work in the most difficult of situations.

They do this because they believe in helping others.

Teaching refugee children about mines on the Kosovo border

Giving food to a school kitchen in Bolivia

Giving medicine to a child in East Timor

Bringing water to children in Zambia

The United Nations works all around the world

Children are the losers in wars.

These little girls are refugees. They are being cared for by the United Nations, until they can go home.

These little girls are in a refugee camp
until it is safe for them to go home

In Angola I met boys who had lost their parents
in the war there.

They sang:
"We are children and we need a mother who hugs us.
What can you do about that?
We are children and we need a father who takes care
of us.
What can you do about that?
We are children and we need to go to school.
What can you do about that?
We are children and we need a childhood.
What can you do about that?"

Painting by a child showing the horrors of war

The United Nations tries to stop wars and
sometimes sends out peacekeepers.

The United Nations peacekeepers are called
Blue Berets and Blue Helmets.

They are soldiers from many countries around
the world.

They are sent out to keep peace,
not to make war.

Some have lost their lives.

Protecting a child in the Democratic Republic of the Congo

Giving first aid in Haiti

Bringing a child back home in East Timor

Teaching how to remove mines in Cambodia

United Nations peacekeepers help in many ways

Children are also affected by poverty.

Poverty is not having enough to eat.

Poverty is not having decent housing.

Poverty is not having medicine when you are sick.

Poverty is having to work instead of going to school.

Nearly half the world's population lives on less than two dollars a day.

The United Nations fights poverty.

This little girl carries her brother
through a garbage dump looking for food

To fight poverty people need to be able to work.

This is a wonderful honey-making school in Ghana.

People were taught everything about honey-making.

Then they could go home and earn money.

The man to the left kept chanting:
"Honey-making, money-making."

Here I am with a group of honey-makers in Ghana

Children need to go to school so that they have a chance to do what they want to do in life.

Millions and millions of children around the world are not in school.

This little boy has to work instead of going to school. He has fallen asleep over the softballs he has to make.

Almost two-thirds of the children not in school are girls.

The United Nations is working to make sure that every child can go to school.

This little boy has fallen asleep while making softballs

I remember the war widows I met in Guatemala.

They wanted their children to go to school.

With the help of the United Nations they formed a weaving group.

They wove beautiful textiles to sell to help pay for the school.

Meeting the children in Guatemala

In India I visited a school for poor children set up by a young woman.

I came to a wall and a door in the wall.

It was opened by a smiling young woman. Behind her I saw all the children dressed in red gym clothes.

I asked one of the little girls what she wanted to be when she grew up. She said with glittering eyes: "A doctor."

Through education you can realize your dreams.

I didn't take a camera along,
so I made this picture for you!

I hope that you also believe in working for
a better world:

>a world without war;

>a world without hunger;

>a world without poverty;

>a world where children can be happy.

The little things in your own life are also IMPORTANT:
like saving water or electricity, or helping out a
friend in trouble.

My husband often says: "The world is not ours to
keep. We hold it in trust for future generations."

AND THAT IS YOU!

A hug!

The book has been made possible by a gift from the Boorstein Family Foundation in memory of Pauline Fox Boorstein, an early supporter of the United Nations Association of the USA. Profits from the sale of this book will be donated to UNICEF

Copies are available from:
The American Forum for Global Education
120 Wall Street, Suite 2600
New York, NY 10005
(212) 624-1300
Visit our Web site: www.globaled.org

Credits as follows • Front Cover and page 31: Illustration by Nane Annan • Page 3: United Nations/UN Photo by Y. Nagata ARA • Page 5: Photo by W. Ball • Page 9: UN/DPI Map by Bernhard H. Wagner • Page 13: UN/DPI Photo by Evan Schneider • Page 15: *upper left*: UNICEF/HQ99-0494 Photo by Jeremy Horner; *upper right*: UN/DPI Photo by Greg Kinch; *lower left:* UN/DPI Photo by Eskinder Debebe; *lower right*: UNICEF/HQ96-1166/Photo by Giacomo Pirozzi. • Page 17: UN/DPI Photo by Eskinder Debebe • Page 19: UNICEF/C115#17 • Page 21: *upper left*: UNATIONS; *upper right*: UN/DPI Photo by Eskinder Debebe; *lower left:* UN/DPI Photo by Eskinder Debebe; *lower right:* UN Photo 159491/J. Bleibtreu • Page 23: UNICEF/HQ99-0808 Photo by Roger Lemoyne • Page 25: UNIC/Ghana Photo by Margaret Novicki • Page 27: UNICEF/HQ89-0052 Photo by Gilles Vauclair • Page 29: UN/DPI Photo by Evan Schneider • Page 33: UN/DPI Photo by Marcia Weistein (NJ) • Back Cover: UN PHOTO 145618 Photo by John Isaac: The UN Flag